Spi ... en's ...

 LONDON BOROUGH OF
RICHMOND UPON THAMES

D1494708

Russell Punter

Illustrated by David Semple

At mighty Cobweb Castle,
there lives the Spider Queen.

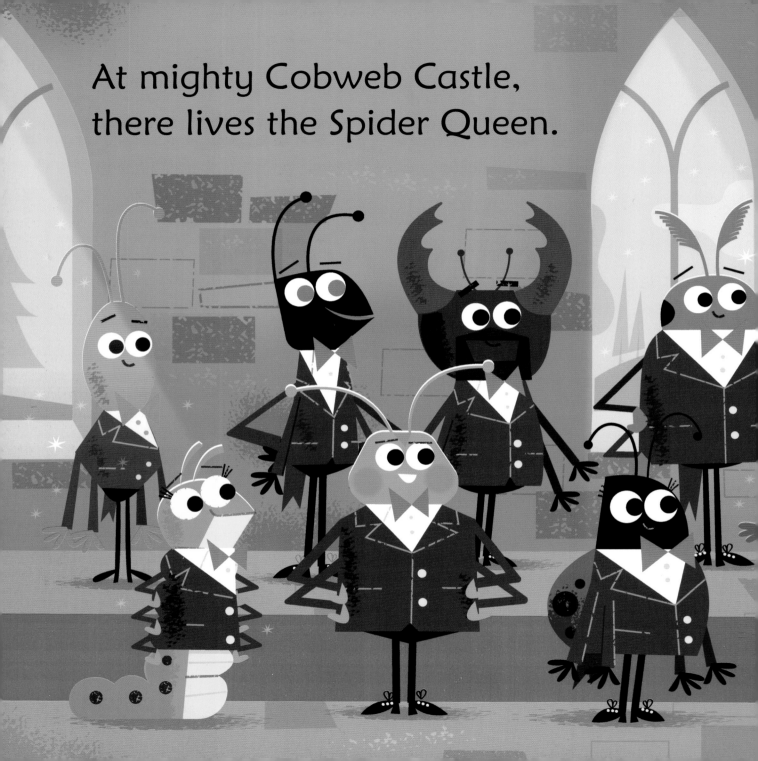

"We'll get things ready,"
Weevil says.

Well please don't let me down.

"Let's get beetling," Weevil calls, lining up his team.

They hang up creepy streamers
that dangle in the breeze...

then carve out eerie pumpkins
and perch them in the trees.

They make some spooky cookies
and shakes that look like slime.

They carry out a barrel
for apple bobbing fun.

At last, their job is done.

The Spider Queen comes sprinting out, her face lit up in glee.

Oh no! She slips upon a blob of slime and slides into a tree.

A pumpkin drops SPLAT on her head.

I can't see where to go!

She lands inside the barrel.

SPLASH!

It's all gone wrong.

OH NO!

Her face paint slowly dribbles down.

That's not the Spider Queen!

"Rewards for all who caught the thief!
What brilliant bugs you've been."

About phonics

Phonics is a method of teaching reading which is used extensively in today's schools. At its heart is an emphasis on identifying the *sounds* of letters, or combinations of letters, that are then put together to make words. These sounds are known as phonemes.

Starting to read
Learning to read is an important milestone for any child. The process can begin well before children start to learn letters and put them together to read words. The sooner children can discover books and enjoy stories and language, the better they will be prepared for reading themselves, first with the help of an adult and then independently.

You can find out more about phonics on the Usborne website at **usborne.com/Phonics**

Phonemic awareness

An important early stage in pre-reading and early reading is developing phonemic awareness: that is, listening out for the sounds within words. Rhymes, rhyming stories and alliteration are excellent ways of encouraging phonemic awareness.

In this story, your child will soon identify the *ee* sound, as in **Queen** and **Halloween**. Look out, too, for rhymes such as **slime** – **time** and **team** – **scream**.

Hearing your child read

If your child is reading a story to you, don't rush to correct mistakes, but be ready to prompt or guide if he or she is struggling. Above all, do give plenty of praise and encouragement.

Edited by Lesley Sims
Designed by Hope Reynolds

Reading consultants: Alison Kelly and Anne Washtell

First published in 2021 by Usborne Publishing Ltd., Usborne House, 83-85 Saffron Hill, London EC1N 8RT, England.
usborne.com Copyright © 2021 Usborne Publishing Ltd.